THIS VANISHING

This Vanishing

Poems by Dave Caserio

CW Books   Cincinnati   Ohio

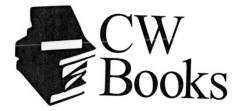

© 2014 by Dave Caserio

Cover art: Michael Zansky, *Thought Transference*
Cover design: Pete Tolton
Author photograph: Jessica Jane Hart
Layout: James Hickman

Published by CW Books
P.O. Box 541106
Cincinnati, OH 45254-1106

Poetry Editor: Kevin Walzer
Business Editor: Lori Jareo

ISBN: 9781625490919
LCCN: 2014943341

Visit us on the web at www.readcwbooks.com

For Muriel and Richard

Acknowledgments

Grateful acknowledgment is given to the publications in which the following poems, some in slightly altered versions, first appeared:

Salmon: "Muriel" and "Mecca"
This Order: "Dublin Station"
Crab Creek Review: "In Memory of Jeremiah Buck,"
    "Ghost Eye" and "First Sunday In New York,"
Footwork: "How Close the Child to the Skin" and
                "Body"
Children Remember Their Fathers (Anthology): "My
    Father Used to Stay Up Nights"
Live! The Seattle Poetry Slam CD: "Forensic Love"
*Poems Across The Big Sky: An Anthology of Montana
    Poets:* "Chicago, 1959"
The Montana Arts & Culture Magazine: "Turin, Italy,"
    "Vermont Etiology," "A Terrible Music," and
    "Catherine"
Stones Throw Magazine: "Chicago, Year's End"

Many thanks to Bart Baxter, Sylvia Caldwell, Cara Chamberlain, Martin Farawell, Ed Kemmick, and Catherine Martin-Darby, who read early and late versions of this work and to Kevin Walzer, Lori Jareo, and WordTech Communications for making this book possible. A heartfelt thanks and appreciation to John Moriarty and Andrea Seals for their art and friendship. My thanks to James Hickman for layout and technical support, to Jessica Jane Hart for author's photograph, and to Pete Tolton and Michael Zansky, for cover design and cover art. And a special thanks to Tami Haaland for furthering the work of so many.

Contents

IV

V

VI

I

... Posterity has no use
For anything but the soul.
The lines that speak the passionate heart.
The spirit that lives alone.

Patrick Kavanagh

Forensic Love

I will be unearthed—
Another nameless coffin in an overcrowded world
In 2098—and they will jettison me ninety-two million,
Eight hundred and twenty-seven thousand miles
Beneath the sun, unto the eternal revolving wheel.
Bin of old bones that once in vacuum will never die
But spin in contrapuntal harmony with the moon.
Dark sister may she last, watching as I watch,
Whatever earth, with each unfutile spring, may bring
Again: great grey heron rising from pure blue of water
Out over mist and reeds, or redwing blackbird, first seed
And thorn, or Copernicus to tell us he was wrong;
That the human heart and not the sun
Marks the center, the doorway to life.
And perhaps this end will not be the end.
But nicked by a meteor, thrown by its wake,
This ole jangle and clank of bones
With their endless code of once living
Cells of experience will, as a wolf howl
Or a vowel will, without the consonant of things,
Drift toward the vast outer unknown.
Unlured by Saturn, uninjured by the sun,
Able to miss each wandering asteroid
As ancestors, sister and brother to my uncle
Joe Vezzetti—long may his gold tooth gleam
—did not. For in a moment of singing they failed
To miss, and travel on their way, a careening
Drunk one night on a mountainside road in Italy.
And before bursting in smithereens, they went
Screaming into flames. But I will last until I last,
Bump up and nuzzle the nose of another someone
Who, in whatever form, will pluck me from the deep.
Mystery or fraud, I will be as Lucy from Olduvai Gorge,
Piltdown Man, mask of Agamemnon or whatever hunkered
Unknown daubed a bison's soul in primordial light of
Lascaux. Here the knee bone slipped the femur, the tibia
Twisted away, the shin scraped and the toe cracked.
But not the how or why, not the song. Not that I was drunk

And spinning on one leg, whirling as if it were a stick of
Fire above my head a cherry-red, feedback engorged,
Eight-stringed electric bass guitar that yowled and
Screeched, shrieked as shrieking cats in heat or wild Picts
At Hadrian's Wall, when I tripped and fell and broke my
Damn knee. So perhaps, bit by bit, those who discover me
Will come to know what fragrance lies unbloomed.
What Bushman chant or Ibo tongue?
What vanished larynx of Sioux?
What grief Enkidu under earth?
Upanishad, or Andromache at the wall?
Odysseus before the blood?
Or Gullah, Geechee, a south side jive?
What palaver we, as humans are,
That lingers in these bones.

II

What is the price of Experience? Do men buy it for a song?
Or wisdom for a dance in the street?

William Blake

How Close the Child to the Skin

Please, No!   Please, Daddy!   Daddy, Please Don't!
Wailed a voice like an animal caught in a trap.
I turned right there on the corner of 51st & 9th
Into the swift glare of car hoods and sunlight,
In front of the red awning of Arriba Arriba,
Before the Afghan eatery, and saw a woman
Weeping, mumbling, against the chest of a man.
But there was no tension between them,
Only her complete willing collapse.
Then she wailed again.
And I was six or maybe seven.
And *Daddy, Please Don't* was as helpless in me
As when he beat my mother or sat there
In the alcohol of his own weakness and pain;
Or when I threw myself between the slapping,
The punching, the swearing, the knife. Now
On this street how this woman's voice held
My voice, note for note, tenor for tenor,
Until the child rose up in me squawking and howling
That it was not all done, that it had come again.
And I stood there through a shaking so abrupt, as if
The covers had been torn from the clammy chill of fever.
I wanted to roll back underneath into the damp and dark
But rose instead, in some ghoulish attempt at light,
And took from the ground that six-year-old-child, and
Knew only, that I could not bury him again.

Muriel

My mother held out for tangerines.
They were more willing than the orange,
Rare as China, still, and carried the
Thought, which was never spoken,
That life was no more than that.
Peeling them now in the darkened
Kitchen, the taste of them almost in
My mouth. A mouth forged
From the soft melding of two others
Slipping open like caves found
In darkness, moistening the sweet,
Heavy air that fell between them
With the thought that was never spoken.
My thumbs enter the skin
No differently than did those
On the hands of my father
Unbinding slowly,
For the first time, her shoulders
More willing than oranges,
And found a fruit,
Rare as China, still.

Chicago, 1959

Through the hot summer twilight
Just this edge of light
I would rest in the bodies
Of my father, grandfather,
Uncles Tony and Joseph,
On one lap or another
Like the small animal I was.
My face a pebble under
A wood-dark stream
As my lungs released
Cricket by cricket
Into the slow exhilaration
Of a falling sky
As a yellow-bulb
Lantern frame dipped in
And out of my eyes
Swaying as a boat sways
Across the unmeshed
Darkness of the sea.
And I was drawn,
Tenderly as blood,
Through the rhythms of their flesh
And the unspoken womb
Of the company of men.

Orphans

Four years old
Timid in the bathroom,
The question Adam most likely
Asked of Eve, I asked of my mother,
"What's it for?"

I think of the treetop
Full with blackbirds
Caught between the ridges
Of her thighs.

Thick, circular, black,
It wasn't a mustache like Chaplin's
Or heart-shaped, close-cropped,
But rounded—double-barrelled,
Orphan Annie peeping out from
The cervix:
Calling me.
The way a half open
Cellar door takes
One down.

And I remember her peeing.
A slim sound—like runoff
Falling across the moist fallow
Of a drop-back cave.

Almost squatting she was
Willful as a she-bear;
But small, thin. Her
Pelvis tipped back and up.
Legs turned out surrounded
By pajama bottoms.
Hair, blueblack
Across the white blouse hung
On the hanger of her shoulders.

And I fell into a curious love.
I fell and didn't know I had fallen,
Leaning there like rubber

Against the porcelain sink, coy
And cute as I could muster, lost
In a way I have never
Quite been able to recover.

I Dreamed Owls

Three owl chicks and the mother flying home,
The night Reggie disappeared.
We still had firecrackers, cherry bombs and M-80's.
All our parents sat on porch steps,
The deep-drag, red coal tips of cigarettes,
The quick glare of aluminum under lamplight,
As they pulled down beer after beer
Along that August edge, on that south side Chicago.

Miz Hattenbach, the humpbacked crone of seventh grade,
Visioned out of crab weed and dandelion,
Hovered in the torpid weary air of prairie heat.
While under the torqued summer weight of trees
Coco, my brother Don, Dennis, and Lithuanian Charlie
Played baseball—all day—at Palmer Park.
Pullman trains over Pullman tracks.
And the vegetable man, his sweet corn tomatoes
Sweet corn potatoes, sweet corn before evening.
And the white mosquito truck,
Into whose fog-bank of chemical spray
We swooped, pedaled our bikes and breathed deep.
Already, we'd begun to shrink, every vowel
Squeaking down until we were the size of elves or worse
Withered into the kingdom of cicadas, porous among
The trees. Abuzz in our parents' ear: "I scream. I scream.
Aw give the kids ice cream."

But some fool kid shrieked from his bike,
Tumbled out of the white cloud,
A spurt of bone
Through the skin of his wrist.

And then the fun was over.

Except for Dale,
Who dropped two fistfuls
Of hoarded-since-last-Fourth-of-July

Gunpowder into an open prairie-lot fire.
Into the white flash went eyebrow and eyelash,
As we teased him home: "Hey Godzilla breath.
Tweet. Tweet. Look at the Birdie."
While he spit and spit at the red-tipped
Coals of his scorched-black fingers.

My father caught us blowing firecrackers at the curb,
Flapped toward us, arms angled, pelican awkward,
And slurred, "Man, feel that breeze. Sure cools the pits."
"Uh, yea," we said, dropping two cherry bombs instead
Through the open sewer grate. "Hey dad, put your
Head down here. These crackers really light it up.
You can see to the bottom, even underwater."

And we waited as he wobbled on curb edge
In a stupor of curiosity—waited for the puckered flash,
For the eruption of silt and black worms.
But somebody yelled, "Reggie's vanished."

My Father Used to Stay Up Nights

My father used to stay up nights
After the midnight shift in the mills
While we three kids half-slept
Waiting for his sweaty, oil-soaked scent.
Our mother not knowing which man
Would come home, or when.
But drunk or sober,
Beer in hand, silhouette at the door,
He'd look in on us.
Our eyeballs fluttering under skimpy
Lids, like heartbeats.
And he'd count, "one, two, three."
Until somewhere in the night
A strange music matching a howl
A hunkering down, a great surging
Out of gut vowels would erupt.
And I would slip from bed
Into the dark stream of the hallway;
The creak of wood he could not hear.
And each time I would see
Where my father sat, legs spread,
White as marble, old as Heraclitus,
Skinny and hairy in his boxer shorts,
The quiet fur of his belly hanging over,
And a clarinet, sometimes a saxophone, wailing,
Blowing that root-reed till the reed cried
Egyptian Mama you make me bleed,
Wailing the Harlem shuffle, Benny Goodman,
Charlie Bird or somebody, anybody.
And all the pain—his father who tied him,
Beat him, and locked him for days in the attic closet,
Once with a sickle splitting him
From forearm to wrist; no future, the mills;
Then the daughter that he would take to bed,
And the wife he would beat senseless, or sons
Already turned away that would never come back—
Maybe, just maybe, finding its way out.

Ghost Eye

My mom woke me
At the foot of the bed
In the middle of the night—didn't
Say Mo, Muriel, or bye.
My eyes went right through her
To the wall, to the TV.
The next day the phone rang and rang.
I wouldn't answer—I made your father
When he came home from work.
I could never lie to her.
She had the eye.
Even the neighbors
Back in Warrington
Waited with their tea leaves.
She'd hold hands and tell
What would happen today, tomorrow.
But her eyes failed, too.
She scrubbed other people's floors until
She was eighty; until cancer and cataracts;
Until she couldn't eat or see.
Doctor Packo says I need to gain some weight.
I'm only eighty-seven pounds,
But my mom was itty-bitty. She was petite.
When the school nurse hit me, said I lied and stole,
Sent me home, she marched me back and told
The nurse that if she raised her hands again she'd cut 'em
Off and the nurse could learn to knit with the metal
Stumps they'd give her. Every payday when I was
Pregnant with you darling, the paycheck, your father,
And the car, were gone to the tavern, to the bowling
Alley, 'til Monday when he'd work the second shift.
Our landlady had a key. She used to steal
Meat out of the icebox. One night I woke up.
She was in my room looking for money, I think. I jumped
Up and slapped her. Said I'd kill her if she came back.
I was scared. I didn't know what to do.
Your father tells me to be strong.
He says he'll be my eyes.

Doctor Packo calls me his little soldier.
Your brother won't look at the hole
Where my eye used to be. It bothers me.
People stare. Everybody
At home in England calls and says,
"Poor Muriel." I'm not
A kid. If I was it would have been
Alright. A few blotches on the skin.
An itchy rash. But it wasn't.
It was Shingles at fifty-eight.
The virus stayed inside and ate
Everything. The doctor said
The back of my eye was Swiss
Cheese. And antibiotics or no
It's still in me and can drift
Into my spine or lodge in my heart
And chew me into a cripple or chew
Me into the grave.
Five surgeries. Six months. And all
Packo gives me is a silver Mylar balloon
Because he ran out of gold stars. I know
He saved my life. Both eyes would be gone if it wasn't
For him. The other doctor misdiagnosed. For two weeks
He said infection and smeared cream in my eye.
At the DMV I couldn't read the top line. It turned
Into alphabet soup. They wouldn't let me
Drive home. Said I was legally blind.
Packo put me in the hospital that afternoon.
I was in surgery the next. I asked,
What if I came to him earlier, could
He have saved the eye? He wouldn't look at me. He said,
"Let's not dwell on what could have been. What's past is
Past." When I was little in England
In the war, my brother Jimmy would go AWOL.
They'd come after him and my mom would have to hide
Him in the garbage. I'd climb on top and bang
The can with my heels and pound. "Hey Garbage!
Get yer fresh garbage! Ooh...
It stinks! Officersergeantsir, could you
Help me lift it to the alley?"
"Never you mind!" She'd say,
And bolt her eyes right through me.
But Jimmy was a paratrooper—

A turret ball gunner in the Royal Air Force.
It wasn't fighting he was afraid of,
It was just a day off now and then that he wanted.
And I don't want to be blind, but I can do it.
I can look into the empty socket in the mirror
And I know I can't look back. But something's still there
When I turn the eye to see.
The muscles move, or feel like they do.
The doctor just shrugs and says, "Ghost eye."
I told your father, "I'll be my own damn eyes."
I don't want him driving me, waiting on me.
The only time he pays attention is when I'm sick.
Otherwise, about the best he does is promise
And buys me another dress or some knickknack.
On the train back from Vegas
The waiter brought fish your father ordered me.
Half my head was still wrapped in bandages,
I looked like a mummy.
And the fish head was still on the fish.
Its eyes were gouged out. Its mouth was open.
I had tea instead. I just wish he'd see,
Just listen to me, talk to me.
When I try to sleep at night I can smell the blood,
See the needle go in,
Freezing the eyeball so the eyeball
Doesn't move while they cut and slice.
They never put me under gas.
They just numbed me
And strapped me
To the table,
Unflapped my eyelids, taped them back.
I could hear scalpels click and scrape.
I could see shadows through the blue gauze
Over my face like the blue paper in my mom's letters.
If you held them up to the light you could see
What was written on both sides. I felt everything
Pouring from me
When they pulled out the eye;
It was still attached.
They just puckered
And popped
It
Out,

Clipped
The
Strings.
I asked if I
Could keep it.
Dr. Packo said: "How?" "Why?"
I said, "In a mason jar
Of formaldehyde on the shelf."
And if Shannon and Kate came for a visit,
If they wouldn't behave, I'd say: "Children,
Do I have to get the eye out?"
On Halloween I'd leave it
In the window in the middle of a pumpkin pie.
When kids came to the door, I'd turn the eye
In the pie so it followed them when they walked.
And I'd cackle: "We got pies for eyes and eyes for pies.
Show me a pie and I'll let ya touch the eye."
Then I'd fling the door open and lift up my patch
And shriek: "Or maybe I'll take yours." But I wouldn't.
I just lay here in bed in the dark. I feel like a ghost.
I keep thinking spiders are crawling from the empty hole;
Or slugs or snakes. The pus runs out all wormy and slimy.
And my cheeks are as sunken as my mother's. But I won't
Take painkillers. What hurts will pass. I dreamed of that
Time where I dreamed I woke your father and drove
To a street in Chicago we'd never seen before.
That time the dog ran away. All the way I kept saying,
"Here. Turn here. Now go straight. See that sign?"
And it happened. Just like I dreamed. When you were
Small. There was Sandy wagging his tail on the corner
And licking our faces. Or that time I pulled a gun.
Gramps was screaming "My House! My House!
I Paid for It. This is My God-Damned House.
It's My Name on the Sonofabitching Mortgage.
Not Yours!" All around the kitchen table his finger
Stabbing at your father, at grandma, at me.
The veins in his neck were purple
And he had spittle coming out of his mouth,
Just like when he died.
I was the only one he'd sit with
After the stroke:
He couldn't stand
Anyone else's company.

He kept weeping and weeping.
I'd make up stories and soothe him
Like one soothes a baby. Maybe we made peace.
But all those times on my hands and knees
Scrubbing their floors, washing their laundry, the way
Your father whimpered around him—I just snapped.
I got so cold inside and I reached into my purse
For that little .22 pistol—The one
Gramps and your father gave me for my own good—
And pointed it at each of them and said, "Okay,
Now whose house is it?" He went white
As the day he died.
He never took his eyes off of me
Just said to grandma, "Sa,
Get your coat; it's time to go."
Honey, everything needs something else.
I don't blame the virus. It did what it did.
But I'm afraid of what I'm becoming.
It's almost funny now. The eye's gone.
The fake one keeps falling out. Yesterday
Little Snowball snapped it up in her mouth.
I only let her out to go to the bathroom, and it rolled
Right out of the socket and on to the ground.
I had to chase her all around the yard.
She kept barking and going into the bushes.
She would have buried it if I hadn't grabbed her.
It's nothing to worry about. But I have to be
Careful. The specialist who made my prosthesis said
It might pop out while I'm asleep. I told him
That's all my husband has to see, an eye
Staring up at him
From the pillow
In the dark
And me
Turned
The
Other
Way.

On the Banks of the Little Thompson River, Colorado

My father wished for cremation. Why?
Perhaps in half memory, in waking dark,
The sliced cadaver, how it was his own life
Would dissect him, admit to the open air
What he could not. The body with its shame,
Erase it. Let the debt be paid another time.

For It Is All Hallows' Eve

And he will not sleep
But wanders the dark.

For I fear that I am he, that man
Ratchet-throated, spigot-voiced,
Squint-eyed, then pop-eyed:
"Whya not ya Wyandot?"

For his wounds are many
And sprout blue flame.

For the blue woad is a fine dye
Outpouring and strong.
But sow near the hive
And the honey shall falter.
Nor will wasp gall be cured from the oak
Or the adder devoured in the ground.
Neither the earthworm come
Willing from the earth.
Yet stain human flesh and the soul
Will rise as Mab to goad Caesar at the shore.

Yet he cannot rise
But howls at the door.

For my father is a platypus
And suffers from figgy tremors.
For his ears fold into hollows.
For his feet and fingers web.
For newborn he flips his tail
Snaps duckling bill at water.
And what sound!
For he is mute and bottom bound.
For fish spine and eel.
For mud worm and grass.
But every morning his breath
Is rot and stink, fishbone and tail,
As he mutters, grits, swallows into waking.

For he hides scissor and razor,
Dreads the fleck, slit, slithe, of a morning's shave,
Will hook no hanger random opposite on a bar
Nor turn a crust of bread upon its side,
But twists all ties, screws all lids.
For what vision will not come
For the spiniferous lip
And spikenard tongue
Of one too long in fire.

For he unsquinnys his eyes with pins
And will not sleep, but slumps at the table,
Mid-finger, then forefinger, fingering
The reluctance of his sex, to rise
As his father made him rise
By harp iron and fire

To be that child who wakes from nightmare sleep:
"Burn me! Burn me!" But not by fire alone.

For I have seen him drunk with a knife:
Dirty pocket, serrated butter, Old Bowie or steak.
First the flat, then the edge, the scratch of the tip
Unearthing the blue vein of the wrist
At the kitchen table at midnight.
For the words of parents, sheathed and unsheathed.
For the ghost of his grandmother who waved in friendless
Thrust: "The Devil will cut your tongue out if you lie."

For he clasps his hand over her mouth
And says nothing upon the crow of his cock
To her dry, shut, sheath.

For my sister must say even less

To the dream of a bloated eyeball
Crammed against a foot,
To a drifting toe and dirty nail,
Or the press of lips on glass,
A float of intestine, a uterine swirl,
A drift of hair, that cries,
"Mother" from a jar.

For the knife is the province of the juggler.
It peels and parries, tips the air
End beyond end,
Palmward then heavenward,
Toward the big-titted,
Star-spangled, fish-netted, spread leg
And spinning woman temporarily forgotten
By the blindfolded blind, as he lets fly for home
The knife into the province of the jugular.

For he hovers against the stove—
The jet of gas, the tickered spark, its blue uproot
Of flame—where his hands play as if music.
They clap and slide and flush with warmth,
Rasp on callous, chime on rings.

For he will open his mouth to hers
A wish of tongue for tongue
Until he thinks she smiles,
And not his thumb, but joy
That pries her teeth apart.

For his knuckles crack. His tendons creak.
For his fingers flit through flame.

For he burps a guttural burp
For the fire belches the same.

For it crinkles the hair of his nose,
Lets it wither and curl and pop.
For it singes eyelash and ashes eyebrow.
And all the length of his arm coils,
Blackens at the blue of his daughter's
Eyes fixed upon the nib of his cock.

Dark, her little weep and gag.

For he stands and urinates
Against what he thinks
Is a toilet, is a wall
At the foot of the stairs,

And every morning the dog is to blame.

For my father being father of the black tar and nicotine.
For my father being father of the delirious whiskey
        numbing.
For my father being father of the diabetic sleep.
For my father being father once child of the whip
        and closet bound.
For my father being father of incest, debt and death
        and faithless vows.
For my father being father, may he wretch the evil away,
May he return to kith and kin.

Let his flesh be perfume and song.

For whatever he has done, has been done,
Has gone and been turned,
In ashes now, turned
To cool waters dreaming.

Body

It is a stain we make
Of the body. The spot,
My sister and I first explored—
Climbing up, one after another,
Before the bathroom mirror
To spread ourselves
Open, front and back,
As one might spread
The gills of a fish
To see how it could breath.

Until a hand
On the door
Pushed
Its way
In, "You kids alright?"

Or after showering
With my father.
His one foot planted,
The other raised
On the tub,
As he toweled
His neck, his chest,
His arms, his legs,
The hairy cheeks
Of his butt
Wobbled
With a humor
I could hardly contain.

So I bent over
To peer up
And in.

But the yell
He let out.

All this
Came back to me

In a stagger
Of electricity,
As I glistened
Under a healer's
Hands.

His thumbs,
Elbows,
Knees,

Digging
And
Pushing

My
Shoulders
Down,
My rib
Cage,
My
Pelvis,

My body
And what
It thought
It was

And what
It was:

A slug
In the wet
Sand that
Knows
No cartilage
Or bone:

Then
First
Mewling
Breath

Of the flesh
Called
Home.

III

I wander thro' each charter'd street,
...And mark in every face...

William Blake

Subway Nocturne

N-U-T-T-I-N!
NUTTIN.
Nuttin, will
Keep me. I
Got nuttin
To do.
Milwaukee
Beer. Old
Brown shoe.
Whisky Comisky.
The old Bronx
Zoo. I got
Nuttin.
Nuttin
To do.

First Sunday in New York

Twenty stories up
I sit on a kitchen stool
With Max, your cat,
Overlooking
The Bronx.
He breathes as I breathe,
Watches as I watch,
The bus gliding down
The perfectly lit boulevard
Where rain seems to flicker
Like firelight pulsing this ecstatic
Flesh, as though it were music
Without sound, silence like fur.
And for a moment the bus is a lantern
Afloat on a dark swath of river
And you still on my tongue
Blossom of orange and sun.
Our eyes paired, stung
By some furor of other blood
Which our bodies trembled in
When in that first mistaken as sin
The unforgotten wonder of origin.

Out Front of Alice Tully Hall

Old bag lady in black shaggy coat:
"Where do the bus go?" The driver
Yells out, "Fourteenth," closes
The door, tries to pull away. But she raps
At him with her gamp. He is gracious. The bus
Dips open. And she steps up scented with oranges.
"Where do it go? This bus used to go clear to Salt
Lake, to the Mormon Temple. I rode it to the River,
To the Angels singing in the desert. Will you take me?"
The driver, perhaps hearing, 'Masonic', says: "Try
Brooklyn." So she turns to her seat on the bench,
As the bus shunts back into traffic, shrugs and begins
To sing: "Hallelujah" "Hallelujah" "Hallelujah".
Her hands lift, fracture side to side, juke, lilt, sway,
As though an absence were filled between them.
As if she were clapping out a song
For all the Angels come
To choir.

Bodega Woman

How many times a day
I gotta do? Lift
This finger. Tap
The keys: Box
Or straight?
80 cent for aspirin.
Beer a dollar cold.
How many cigarettes
I hafta sell
Before my kids get
A better school?
How many times I
Bend my knees, reach
For cartons, whack
For roaches?
How many days
I gotta say:
There's the butter.
There's the eggs.
Cheese?
In the cold-spot
With the milk.
Baby food, yea.
Pajamas, no.
Peanut butter
Cookies,
Suckers 'n'
Chips?
In the back
On the rack.
Protection?
Right in front of ya
Son. Don't be shy.
Better safe than dead.
Now, ya want ribbed
Or unribbed?
Tasty or clean?
'Cause reality

Always comes
With a dream.
So how many
Times a day
I gotta say
In Spanish,
English,
Wobbly Irish,
What we got
And what
We ain't?
My Nona
Came to Little Italy—
Naples to Ellis Island, 1924,
Then here to Hell's Kitchen.
Mom married Irish.
I married Spanish.
That's America.
Nona remembers sharks
When they dumped the dead
Over the side.
Which they weren't
Supposed to do.
But she made the harbor.
She found her way.
And I'm here.
So are the kids.
Dad's down the street
Across from Sonny's
Playing dominoes.
They got beer
And Salsa
Aiyiyian' on
The tin radio.
Plenty of Cuban
Smoke, folding
Chairs: sidewalk
Side with everybody
Walking by.
Whatta ya gonna do?
There ain't no stoop.
But Nona knew a storm
Before it would come.

Her hands would bloat.
Her knees would swell.
But I can't tell
If it's roses or weeds.
Where my kids are going
Or what they're supposed to do,
After 50 cent for candy,
Beer a dollar cold,
Or "How ya want your burger fried?"
Before Mister Death or Mister Tax
Says: "I'll take it all to go."
So I lift these fingers,
Tap the keys,
Box or straight,
And teach my kids the game.
'Cause they'd better know
Each time they bend
If it's ribbed or unribbed,
Tasty or clean.
And which end is giving
And which is getting.

William Cumbry Moss

I used to have it better. I owned three, four
Rooms downstairs at the Baths. A bottle of booze,
Three hours and a girl, only sixty dollars.
You could get girls from Guatemala, sometimes
Other places. Bring them up, pretend to marry,
Make them work for you instead. All they wanted
Was to get in the U.S. But I drank.
I let a cripple into my kip once. He tried to steal,
So I broke his wooden leg. I dragged him out like a dog
With a belt around his neck. I tell him don't touch me
When I'm sleepin'. I jump up quick and cut you.
I tell you even the cockroaches at night wake me up.
So what can you trust about an old drunk? Everything!
Nothing. I got reasons to hate, but I don't. This city will
Wear you smooth, like a stone. A goddamn fossil.
When they found me the last time they put me away.
They diagnosed me as a schizophrenic catatonic amnesiac
And a drunk. Hell, I knew that. They said it'd take me
Three years just to make it back, never mind a job.
But I started chanting. Every day. Every spare moment.
Every block of time. In six months I had a full job
And went back to school. So you tell me. I just saw in
The Post, how Donny Osmond beats depression. He goes
To a nice, quiet spot and reads 'til it's all over.
Only technical books, 'cause if he's going to waste
Time, he should be learning something. To him a novel
Is a waste of time, nothing to learn by it. Well I say,
"FUCK YOU, DONNY OSMOND!"
I say, "God does not abandon negligent men
Who are negligent nor the presumptuous
When they are presumptuous, but he does abandon
The devout man who becomes indifferent, the humble
Man when he is presumptuous. This is what is meant
By sinning against one's condition. From this comes
Dereliction." So says St. Dorotheus. I was
Reading about brains. You know this is all
We got, only so many cells; they don't grow

Back like a fingernail or hair. That's how we get old.
But only male canaries can sing. They learn a new song
Every year. In the spring their brains swell up and all
The old cells die in one particular spot. But they make
More. How? Shit. I don't know. Maybe I can
Do it. Listen, you got a cigarette?

Dipping West at Walsenburg

And it's 8 a.m., Sunday,
November in New York.
This soft-bellied old woman of a dog,
Her delicate milk-sweet lick on my hand,
The dry whisk of her nipples along the curb,
Sniffs, circles, circles, then sniffs again.
While from the corner her owner yells,
With a womanly voice full of steroids, swathed
And wintered in a corduroy sack, harshly,
From a face of sprout and mold:
"Come on...shit. Come on...shit."
And I drop back into memory:
My flushed, three-year-old face,
A plastic rim over a shallow basin,
The knuckle white of the knees,
And the animal grunge rising in my throat.
My father saying, "That's it...come on."
My mother, "Careful...don't hurt."
Except once, going down Highway 25
In a flame-backed Pinto with Illinois plates,
Skimming the Pike Mountains, dipping west
At Walsenburg, under the Sangre De Cristos,
Across the San Juans and down
Into that land that this nation
Threw away with the Navajo and Ute—
Marty and I, three days and sixty joints out
From the hazard waste of Chicago's south side
Where the span between each house
Comes to the shoulder's width of a man;
Where on certain days upon the mercy of the wind
A red dust settles on every crevice, on every sheet
Left hanging, on my old man's new blue Ford, in the hair
And eyes; it grits the tongue and stains a dusky blood
Every neighbor's uncovered pool. So we rolled out at
Twilight on 160 before Teec Nos Pos and Mexican Water,
Ditched the car and skittered like two coyote pups
Yelping all the way up the loose gravel, to the rim
Of the nearest rise, in the basin of the mesas.

And we heard for the first time
Not the squall of a child or sirens
Or old man Vezzetti lost and drunk
Banging on each neighbor's door—
Not even the deathly hum of the mills could touch us—
Only the pure blessed presence of the desert
That filled us with an ancient, shameless, longing
To mark for our own this first mystery of joy,
To howl and kick open the dirt, to shit and howl
To howl and shit, to squat there lifting up
With what was all of our voice
Into that endless rising up of space,
Our frail, human ululation...
The still lingering communion
For all that is alive.

Mecca

Deep in the heart of the perfectly worn boulevards
It is not yet dusk and I am barefoot
In the shrouded rooftops of Hell's Kitchen.
The asphalt stripping is still warm
As I press down and twist my foot
Sideways into the black-bright loam
Which gives way until I too am sinking,
Falling through myself with the weight
Of gold, past the long dead and vacant
Tenement windows, collapsing floor upon
Floor through casements of brick and plaster,
Down into a soft mud-dark.

Building after building
Rolls away in a quiet
Cadence of hills: Soho,
Chelsea, the West Village.
And what seems a tattered
White confetti over the rising
And falling of the city turns
To an endless flocking of pigeons,
A white breathing of bells.

I gaze out as if gazing out over Mecca
And it doesn't matter in which direction I pray
Over this city that is the living animal of man,
The pale enigma of God.

Light
Bursts across chimneys
That swell like teats from rooftops,
Smolders in the cornices of the Ukrainian Church,
The brown brick, red brick, feathers of pigeons,
Grillwork of fire escapes, until it shatters
Across my skull like a crack of gravel dumped
From a wheelbarrow onto a plywood board.
My body bends toward it, like the wound between lovers.
Once, just like this, the way to heaven was clear.

IV

I will not cease from Mental Fight,
Nor shall my Sword sleep in my hand:

William Blake

Vermont Etiology

Since first dark
Only the snow has come
And what would be sound
Is taken back into the body
Like an oar lifted from water.

Except for Moriarty, my friend, and
The private channels of my blood,
I am almost alone.

Each of us shuffles down
The gripless hills,
Like two Poles in Russian winter,
Drawn only by the idea of light
Shining on Montpelier's golden dome,
Haloed in the falling white.

Around blunted corners and back-alley ways,
Through quiet gates of snow,
Through half-covered broken glass
And the rusted time of automobiles,
We make our way—the litter of our
Footprints following like the dead,
The woods so dark on the ridges
In front—until we come
To an old railroad bridge,
Wooden, creaking, still in use.

In the dark
The skelet hands
Of trees
Surround me

As ashen flecks
Melt upon my lips,
Slip across my cheeks,
To the black, unconscious waters below
Where over the world bodies have been offered

From Uganda, El Salvador, Argentina,
From Rwanda, Kosovo, from Guatemala,
The Philippines, Chile, Liberia, Iraq...

They are "the disappeared ones," the estimates,
Figments of imagination,

The slow, the lame, the deemed impure,
The innocent, the dissident, the obstinate,

Who, like
The final, bell-like
Jews, Gypsies, whisper
Without rest as the restless
Water whispers
Beneath this bridge.

Turin, Italy

In the old country up in the north
Where they grow the rice
The second someone dies someone goes
And dresses them, puts them
In a casket or lays them
On a plank, a blanket if they're poor,
Then washes them, hands and feet,
Then sets them in a room, maybe flowers, a rosary.
Some sweet smell for the day when everyone
Comes to see, to eat, to remember
What was once of the body, who it was,
And what it did. And to sit with those
Who cannot yet believe in the weight
Of the emptiness of the body before them.
There are no mirrors in the room,
The windows are shut, the doors closed.
Only the small light of a candle in the evening remains.
And then, except for the mother, the forgetting begins.

Catherine

As if you had died, I walk—
To the market and back again,
To the store for soda pop and paper.
A walking that keeps this weight
Fluid, keeps it from pushing me
Lifeless on the bed. A bed
I cannot roll over on or turn to
Or turn from without reaching
For your small toes, for the deep
Grey and blue of your wolf
Eyes, for hands older than my
Soul, your breath still in me.
Your kisses make me
Forget whether I have a cock, toe,
Belly, hair, form to my fingers;
As if I step from water into air
And cannot tell where it ends or
Leaves, whether I am drinking or
Pouring forth. I cannot walk
To the kitchen or step
From the bath without blundering
Into grief of everything you
Have touched: the small, gold
Box on the shelf; the inkbrush
Of your naked belly and breasts;
Freezer-burst bag of peas, jam
Jar, cups and cream of wheat;
A petite rose's withered spray.
I grieve for the hours when we drift,
Fold and unfold under a murmur of quilt,
Until we curve like a curving moon
To turn the lights and say: "Goodnight.
Sweet Dreams. I love you."
Heart as heart, soul as soul,
Mortal stones in mortal night.

Chicago, Year's End

At 25,000 or 26,000 feet over Cleveland
And Lake Erie, over a sullen watery blotch welling
Into a rim of light, our captain breaks in:
"If you look northward, to your right,
There is a spectacular shot of the Aurora Borealis."
This is the first time in my life to see such a thing.
And I fudge my nose up against the Plexiglas
Just as I would when a child
In the winter-dim light of the Shedd Aquarium
As the dolphin, porpoise, and whale went their liquid ways.
I longed to be that flesh, that oil,
That christened sign of the wave made visible,
To roll in the deep birth moan and rise
On the high, unwinding, undulation of their cry.
But in this season of death,
Of dying and near dying,
Of one friend fallen
And one father falling,
Towards the bitter, holy night
There comes no writhing harp of polar light
Only the pulse-darting flash of wingtip,
A few stars and the general dark.
In which I remember Rexroth's
Love Poems of Marichiko, how the lover's
Tongue thrummed deep into the moist cleft,
Deep into the under-dark,
Yet into radiance they turned,
Into a vast expanding pearl of light:
Lover and Beloved.
And that this is how close I must live my life.
Then kindly it begins—Aurora Borealis—
That careful, lilting hum
Of a pearl being formed.
Slowly, in contagious arcs,
It fills the sky.
And what has been lost
To these mortal hands
Returns.

In Memory of Jeremiah Buck
September 8th, 1834

Flies have tangled and buried themselves
In whatever hair they can find. Eyebrow and eyelash.
Ear gristle and nose. Pine needles rest
Brown amidst the lavender and white of flower.

Only the very old
And very young.

These:
   Olivia,
   Wife of Icabod Dorcas Benton.
     Died, Pittsfield
     May 13th, 1832.

   Or John,
     The second son
     Of Samuel and Olive Wright.
       December 30th, 1832.
       April 15th, 1842.

   And here
   Is William Alden
   The Packard's only son
   Gone at ten months.

Once, I walked in a circle about them
In child politeness taught me
By Aunts in black shawls, in soul deference
Not to step upon their shadows lest they cry out.

Yet now I turn, stubborn against myself,
Chanting with each heavy foot:
Houm
     Houm Kith Kith Kaela Houm
     Kith Kith Kaela Houm Kith
     Kaela huh huh huh huh Houm
     Kith Kith Kaela huh huh huh

3 Stone 3 Stone
Houm Kith Kith Kaela
Modra Faeder Sunu
Faeder Modra Sunu

3 Stone 3 Stone 3

There is nothing left,
Not even memory.

Only this breath
Which drops downward into tree-root and under-dirt,
Long past the rot and mucus, to rest with them
As they bless themselves back into soil and sand and salt,
Back through tree-root, tree-trunk,
Each particle making its way to leaf and bud
Back toward sunlight, toward gaseous spirit,
Toward sun breath

Sunu Modra Faeder
Houm Kith Kith Kaela
Houm Kith Kith Kaela

3 Stone 3 Stone 3.

V

YouFuckersYouFuckersDummyDummyYouDummy
FuckersYouDummyYouDummyFuckers I Get My
Babushka I Get My Babushka YouFuckersYouDummy
Fuckers I Water Your Mouth I Water Your Mouth
I Water Your Mouth With Soap.

   Anonymous

A Terrible Music

When men go to war they break a terrible music
From the air, release the earth her charge of fertility
And nurture into blood-sod and wreck-rhythm, into deep-
Bass pounding of Stuka shriek and screech of shell, of the
Horse-bitted scream and the gritted teeth of wheel-lock
And rail into some great force voiced of their own
They break a terrible music from the air when naming
The names of those pitched from the living, whether
Blameless, or god-favored, frail or wicked, O'Malley or
Juan, Chia or Sean, Gertrude, Helmut, Mohammed,
Louisa, Edgar, eager the blood into the river of dying,
Ever to dark sailing, when men go to war.

Dublin Station

There is a Hearn, an Ahern,
A Barret, a Brit, Burrough,
O'Casey, Connell and Cody,
Dunn and Dundon, Tweet and Twohiss,
O'Callahans, O'Sullivans, six Kellys,
O'Brien, O'Rourke, Smith and Scully,
Murphy and Maycock, perhaps each of the stock
Of the rude fraternity of this morning's
Drunken me'boyo faces on ferry
From Holyhead to Dun Laoghaire,
On bus, now, to Dublin Station.

All night they danced—R&B and Disco,
Soul to Rock 'n' Roll, Euro-Tech, Pop
And Reggae—as they jerked and tupped under laser
Glitter and hull shudder, to the boom-bass hurled
And turgid smash of bow and wave hissing past
Under the lurch and squeak of their crepe-smirched streaks
Across a floor sticky with Budweiser, whiskey and soda.
But there is no flowering wiser in this morning in this year
Of the war in the Gulf—for there is one who was collapsed
In vomit, in the toilet stall; upon whom,
Young girls burst, shrieking: "Where's the Cock?
Come on, don't be shy. Give us a peak a' the beastie thing."
But he heaves as the ship heaves—Whump, Whumph,
Wump, Whumpwhump, as if channel fire—
A thump of guts, splash of water,
"Hey now, stop that puking, and show us your..."

"Cock! Cock! Cock-a-roo! Cock." But the young men
Are chanting now, from the open deck of the
Double-decker bus, down to the young girls below:
"Give us a whiff a' that yeasty bait,"
As we wait in front of the terminal ticket office window:
"And we'll give ya a peek a' the Cock."

Is this how my grandfather went to Gallipoli?
In cock and valor, in lust and song,

By hornpipe bands and their bantering chant,
A bluster of kisses as promises waved at fair dames,
Singing, "Who'll Go a Waltzing Matilda With Me."
And the beribboned flutter of their flags tacked to
Picket boats in line—*The Irresistible, The River Clyde,
The Argyle.* Did he go to those fields of corn, those gullies
Of thyme and red poppies, to rivers of salt and the blood-
Frothed hail of the Turk Ezine, to leap at the Munster's
First charging, of shamrock sprig, of the green and the pale?
Then Dubliners, then Hampshires, crying: "Out Aussies
Of Anzac, Gurkhas and Sikhs. You Lancashires,
Zealanders, Maoris, never retreat!"

So they died on the lighters, over the bloated dead and
Submerged, through the gore of the rocks to the ground
Of the beach, crying "Mother of God" in mother tongue all
The shrieking day of Suvla Bay to Sedd el Bahr.
And even the night: Shouts of, "Allah!"
Screams of, "Christ!" Of, "Hatun, Ana." "Ayo Gorkhali!"
Of, "Ka mate, Ka mate—Ka ora, Ka ora!" You shall die.
You shall die. All of you shall die in the shallow-mouthed
Plains with silver tin plates, in the hills and the knolls
With the shit of the flies, till all death-split tongues
Fold into one. The morning, in the year, Lords Kitchener
And Churchill gave the Turks a peek a' the cock.

But they will not stop, "Cock! Cock! Cock-a-roo Cock!"
Singing: "Tie a yellow ribbon round the old oak tree, the
Old oak tree, the old oak tree. And don't sit under the apple
Tree with anyone else but me, anyone else but me, anyone
Else but me. No. No. No. Don't send me off to Gallipoli.
Take anyone else but me, anyone else but me, anyone else
But me. No. No. And keep me away from Mortar Ridge
Or Shrapnel Valley. And don't be off to Dead Man's Land
Or Bloody Angle, Bloody Angle, Bloody Angle. Unless,
Unless, of course you want to be a putrid slimy sea of
Pustulate flesh, of lice and fleas, of myrtle, mud and gore,
A baking in the sun. Clap. Clap. A baking in the sun.
Clap. Clap. We all go off to No Man's Land,
With whistle and tin we go, whistle and tin we go,
Whistle and tin we go. Clap. Clap. We all stood up and
Over the top, over the top again. Clap. Clap.
Over the top we wend. Clap. Clap.

Over the top again. Clap. Clap. Went the bristle and spin
Of machine gun lead 'til we all fell down dead, all
Fell down dead, all fell down dead. Oh why did I join
The Infantree and the bloody Ar-ar-mee, the bloody
Ar-ar-mee, bloody Ar-ar-mee. Because, Because,
BecauseBecause, Because I was Bloody well barmy,
Bloody well barmy, Bloody well..."

And they clap, and they clap, and they clap again.
"Cock! Cock! Cock-a-roo! Cock!" In the House of Lords,
On the Senate floor, at the Arc de Triomphe and the U.N.
Door. To the deserts of Araby, we shout and sing,
Let freedom ring in this Silver Jubilee of Super Bowl XXV,
As we tie a yellow ribbon round the old flaccid tree
In the year of the war Saddam caught a peek a' the "Cock!

Cock! Cock-a-roo! Cock!" And it's two steps up a time
The conductor comes running: "Who's makin' war-whoop
And racket? Ye ain't goin' to fight.
Ye ain't goin' nowhere—yet.
So have some respect for mother tongue
Or it's off the bus I'll throw ya."

And their eyes slap his back cocksure and grinning like
The eyes of my grandfather and the eyes of those upon
First pink meat of sky over Dardanelles' lavender sheath;
First hurrah and last, rising over the stunned, unearthly
Beauty of wild rose and sage, of olive and thyme, and the
Faint glistening light of cypress and oak, hyacinth and
Grass, winking with spider webs and dew at the bejeweled
Sparkle of the bay; when rose the enormous globe
Of blood-fire over the last faery trace of phosphorous
Green water smoothed into a glassy, oily sea—
Surface of black eyes: a thousand ruptured fish aglitter.

Then the tidbit flecks of rifle fire,
The scintillating wobble of bayonets,
And the empty gauntlet of eyes'
Horizon-ward stare through the nothing
Between them and the pouring dead
Oozed in runnels of cankerous tongues
And gangrenous arms; legs a bag of mush.
Rain soaked, frozen, then rained again,

They shudder in their own fly-buzzed clouds of shade
At the loveliness of Troy and snowcapped Samothrace,
Before Imbros' jagged scrim, crown of Tenedos,
Upon the ships' transfigured faces,
The stink of burning dead:

Through the hills of Gallipoli, in my land and yours,
In the deserts of Kuwait, by the waters of Babylon, in
The first holy cities, upon the flesh of mother tongue,
Cry: "Mam", "Ma", "Mutter", "Modra", "Mater",
"Mere", as all matter cries when first torn asunder.

"Cock! Cock! Cock a..." But the conductor turns
As my grandfather turned, in silence, to pints and sausage,
And spits: "Don't ye dare.
Not another fokkin' word, ya fokkin' bloody bastards."

It Was Always Errol Flynn

And when he played General George Armstrong
Custer in, *They Died With Their Boots On,*
And when Crazy Horse thundered across
The sharp grass of Little Big Horn hill,
He held what earth was his.

And whooped and tangled on a prairie lot,
Wedged between Pulaski's shack and the alley,
With little Paulie scalped and Kenny filled with arrows,
Or Benteen miles away or trapped and gutted, I stood
Flushed in the spirit-filled air, my imagined hair
Fluttered and gold as the feathers of the coming lances.

VI

The lyf so short, the craft so long to lerne,
Th'assay so hard, so sharp the conquering,
The dredful joye, that alwey slit so yearne,
Al this mene I by Love.

Geoffrey Chaucer

What Angelina Madonna Said at Ninety-Two When Asked, "How Was Death?"

Dust? How was dust explained to me?
Well, Monroe, Kansas, was dusty, and Corona too.
New Mexico was filthy coal dust, ash, and soot.
It gritted the air and tasted like burnt toast.
Nobody had to go down no shaft. They washed that
Coal right from the hills, with hoses and dynamite.
It dusted over everything like a sprinkle of gunpowder.
I couldn't have a cup of coffee or a plate of stew
Without my brothers, Pete and John, trying to light my
Vegetables with a match or hissing at me like little Tony
Bellini Braccacia and his cousin Luchesca would
Whenever they said, sassafras or succotash. What I ate,
I ate cold, afraid it would catch fire or explode.
One time Pete or maybe John dropped a crawdad in my
Supper. I didn't see it on the spoon. It clutched my tongue
Like a scorpion. Like the one that skittered out of the pail
And got Ma when Ma got water and bit her.
I gagged it up, a mush of mash-potato, carrots and peas.
It splat on the mat, wiggled, and started to crawl after Pa.
He just laughed and knuckled it off the table.
That time John and Pete turned yellow
There was black scum on their lips. They said, 'Maybe
It's the water.' And Pa said, 'Maybe it's the air.' But
Ma hushed. She knew they'd been smoking coffee grounds
And crazyweed, drinking root liquor, out behind the hill.
Which is where Pa would have buried them if he caught
Them. But Kay and I would play with the weeds that grew
By the fence. We'd braid them like hair, stick them on
Popsicle sticks, make lips with lipstick and eyes with dirt.
We'd give them names, tell stories, and have tea
With the mud. When the trains would go by, we'd watch
The boxcars like kids watch TV. There were pigs and
Hobos, and men with guns, Texas way to the Rio Grande,
Down to give Old Pershing a hand to save them sissy
Texans from Villa's Band. And we saw a man plucking
A chicken and eating it raw. One time the elephants went by.
There was one sad lonely eye through the slats
Where the snuff of their noses with holes like

Figures of eight would take peanuts from your fingers.
The ballerinas had puffs of hair that sparkled with candy
Canes and feathers. They tiptoed and spun on the galloping,
Bare backs of horses, while a spinning, spangled, armless
Man caught knives with his teeth, and the tigers roared,
And the clowns fell, and the Ringmaster said,
"Dear Angel, step up out of the dust and join the show,
Cause we're going to Baltimore and Kansas City Mo."

Where There is a River as This

I.

Where there is a river as this
 every particle of crap blood-washed and blood-lined.
Where the dead lung of water and the death bellied carp.
Where the river does not glide of its own sweet will
 but frets and gluts.
Where the brown sick foam of the Illinois cataracts
 under Starve Rock—whirls with the Ohio toward the flank
 of the Mississippi.

Where the Illiniwek would not come down but left their
 bones and their children to the dirt-pine and nests of birds,
 to the black-suet, berry seeded shit of bears. Starve Rock.
Over whose edge my father held me be-hawked and
 un-hooded, to clip the dove or talon the pike,
 tight in plummet, wide-swung in wonder.
My father held me, birded and preying,
Over water that no man gives but takes.

II.

"Blind in blind wilderness,
Flash flood,
Hail, wind, rain,
I thought Clark dead.
Only our luck,
Only our perseverance,
Allowed us to live,
To go on naming:
The Dearborn, the South fork
Colt Killed Creek, River Philosophy,
The Dog, the Bull, Teapot and Wisdom.
For we made the Panther into the Pipe-Stove.
For the Bitter-Root became Quick Sand.
Elk Rapids our Linchpin and Half-Breed.
For the Judith, wide and timbered—box elder,
Cottonwood, rose bush and honeysuckle.
For Clark's wife this sweet naming.

But Flathead, we kept...
Though they called it, 'Koos-Koos ke'
Or, 'clear water running'."

III.

Steady flush of blood and matter, the fevered, pustular
 phlegm: hooves, heart, brains, belly, kidney, liver and
 lungs, tail, tongue, and tripe, oil and fat, hide and hair.
Beef-cows of the five great plains.
Sweet-bread of thymus, weasand and snout.
The un-cadenced moan of the stunned calf's skull,
 gelatinous eye in a skim of grease.
Bubbly Creek:
A meat-spackled slime, slop of testicle and ovary,
 crushed trachea and bone;
Of water once water no more:
 chlorinated, sulfuric, ammonia and lead,
 sweet odor of molasses.

IV.

Where Potawatomi, Ottawa, Chippewa, deer and grouse—
River of steep hands and sweet marsh.
Where glacial waters ran, down Wolf Ridge, in Panhandle
Wood where cholera woman wanders bald and virgin.
For it is night on the river dead.
Its liquid ventriloquism of light
Through fog and lowland mist, in the whisper
Of plank and barrel, bobbing in regurgitant debris,
In factory and fractured hull, in rust, in ice.
But no dog tooth. No willow.
The cypress gone.

For a river went out of Eden
For man to dress and keep:
For the Pi son of Havilah is of gold and bdellium,
 onyx the stones on its shore.
For second is Gihon that compasseth Ethiopia.
Eastward, the heart of Hiddekel.
Fourth, Euphrates.

Tell me where
Is there a river as this.

Maybe It's Mustard or Maybe It's Jam

Hey, I wasn't one of those kids
       that put peanut butter
             in your shoes
Just to make you think, or squeezed
       the frog's head into your glass of milk.

And I never reached into my nose and pulled
       out a string of gangrenous green
Just to see
       what color you'd turn. But I gotta tell ya now
How Little Paulie's stool was creamy soft and seemed
To go on forever—like the Tastee Freeze would if they
Forgot
      to push
           the
               lever
                   back
                     up.
          All puppy brown not chalky
                   white or
One of those dark elbows floating at the bottom of the toilet
       in a halo of rich green silt
                or
                 the stringy pulpy
Kind that won't wash away
Flush after flush. Now I don't like wiping
It off my shoe anymore than you and wondering
If maybe it's mustard or maybe it's jam; but I never
Learned to fear what we all do. Hell, even
The Mongol Emperor sniffed the bit from his
Mongol son: less meat, more porridge, add some
Greens and cut down on the yak butter.
                     'Cause

What we delete is what we eat;
    And well chewed is well spewed.
       It's the same as saying, "Salude", to your health.

How do you think we used to find food?
               Follow the shit

And you'll find the food.

Wild turkeys leave crude, "J's".
Even the gentle, English Badger
Offers up a daily potpourri
of where he has been and what
he has done.
Grizzlies leave sloppy muddy blintzes
The size of a 47 odd shoe.
But hey, I didn't
Bring this up.
Little Paulie's dad Big Paulie
Did,
down in the basement trying to rectify his own
troubles.

He had that coconut—which we thought
Looked like a jumbo woolly mammoth's nut—jammed
In a vise,
and was whacking it with a hammer;

But it wouldn't budge. This:
"somnabitchinthickskinnedfuckinfruit!"
Then he got his hacksaw.
Which worked.
But the juice started dribbling down the side and on
to the rusty blade.
So, Big Paulie grabbed some nails instead
And started tapping them in on top.
When he was finished, it was
A voodoo head with spikes:

"Oh Boy, we'd drink this stuff in the Navy,
in the Philippines, with rum and whiskey, or
bathtub hootch.
But, too much a' this stuff will give ya the diarrhea."

And all the while, Little Paulie
Was drinking milk and shoving
Oreo cookies down his craw.

But that wasn't the real problem.
It was his kid and he should have known

What that kind of talk would do.

Because God knows
        what that poor child was eating
                all morning we were down
                        in the ditch that used to be

An Italian-Polish neighborhood and was
Going to be the future Dan Ryan Expressway.
But now was nothing but
A big looping, muddy hole 'round the south side:
Full of empty cans and empty boots,
Snakes and worms, bricks and snails, spiders and weeds,
And left over cheese sandwiches in soggy brown
Bags—whatever people threw down or crawled in
And couldn't crawl out.

By the time we left
Little Paulie had more mud around his mouth
Than Nebuchadnezzar had grass stains on his knees.

Big Paulie barely got him up
Five flights of stairs, through three doors
And four slippery rugs, before toilet paper was flapping

Off the hook,
And he was cursing
his own damn mouth.

Like I told ya,
It all comes down
To shit.
Whether
Fibrous
And damp,
Mushy or
Firm,
Black
As sin
Or grey
As an old
Lover's eyes.

'Cause everything eats everything else, so
We're all shit in the end anyway.

And in the mortal words of that great American bard WW,
        "We grow such sweet things out of such corruptions."
For earth "gives such Divine materials to men
                and accepts such leavings from them at last."

                So Praise Shit!
                Canonize Scat!
                And Sing!

Like we sang all that day
Up and down east a hundredth street
From Michigan to State.

                "You're a Poopcake Man.

                Yes, I am.

Maybe it's mustard.   Or maybe it's jam.

                Shaddup."

This Vanishing

Corings from Alerce trees unstumped and still standing
  yet in Chile, in Argentina, tell us 3,613 years of human
    rage, of human love, ferocity and power, of fury,
      silence, and perhaps of mercy, have mattered
        only a little; almost nothing: a tattered ozone,
      a leak of radiation, to the long arc of seasons.

Yet from continental divide to southern tropic, from northern
  lights to Hawaiian forests, less and less of the aster,
    cypress and elm, of the rufous towhee or the fustic
    wood, of wrasse and wren, of vicuna and vole,
      of the brook trout and the garpike, the black mouth
      chinook or the urchin, the shrike and the shrew,
        from slow worm to burning blue wahoo, or from
        a zoophagous opossum to a custard ylang-ylang,
      are left to be or be imagined.

And this leaving without trace; no line in the dirt
  that we will not cross into hurricane and wildfire.

And this vanishing, this nothinged embrace, could be
  a divine sanction or a rock rattling an empty can.

For what holds us is so slim; a degree
  or two colder, a touch of heat, and it might
    as well be Mars.

So perhaps Mr. Clarke did not write science fiction, perhaps
  even in the 9 Billion Names of God, nor was the feathered
    serpent tongued Quetzalcoatl science fiction, or the dark
    Kachina god squirming ever into new life, or the song
      of Shiva upon whose exhalations universes are
      sung into being and whose inhalation
        annuls their light.

Just as the final lights were squeezed one by one
  when the last names of God were spun
    by monks in secret naming.

Who witnessed, it seems, each star
 go out, without remorse, with ecstasy
  perhaps, agony for some or melancholy
   and dread; a few resentful, cheated.

And no one there
 after thumb to candle flame
  to watch the last smoke curl
   in quiet into deeper quiet and back
    again after a portion of whatever is time.

In the same way that laughter erupts
 below on 9th Avenue from a pitch of silence,
  a river of horns, from the whoosh and drone
   of cars: a towering, dark-skinned Puerto Rican

Woman screams in Spanish, in English, curses,
 swings her aluminum bat flashing
  like a silver dagger at a man
   who dodges, stumbles over garbage,
    then rolls with a scatter of beer bottles
    that skitter into a screech of traffic.

"Chinga Tu Madre!"
   He stands in headlights and dust.
"I cut you, you bitch!"

And he stares into eyes of death
 as I did once a becalmed day on Lake Michigan
  toppled boatside into clear blue silted green
   sparkle, then nothing, then something, and though
    I could swim dark foreboding rose out of the black
    maw bottom without end, thump of murky Aum,
    first sound and last.

And the icy wilt of all my heart—speck in
 water's vast uncertain if; whether rising
  up or drifting down I screamed, or burbled,
   as though my shadow were shark.

As now her shadow falls across this man
 through a tinkle of bottles and wind.

And he knows as I know, as everyone on the stoop knows
   that what she wishes she will, and he cowers
    as we cower, rain-blind in flood-tide,
     under the lightning and the glory
      at the roiling Mississippi, at
       the squat and venomous Missouri,

For the mud to unchurn, for the waters
   to unswallow, our laughter
    to fail, as she shames him then taunts him

As the police come, chase everyone in
   on this cool July night in New York
    after eight days of one hundred degree swelter,
     after asphyxiation of elderly
      in airless tenements, dogs
       in cars; and now snowfall in Mexico City.

City of breathable shit. Tenochtitlan. Lake of flowers
   and reeds, of torch-light and wild succulent fruit,
    of jaguar and ant.

Now, city of the future world, what are we naming?

Does the wise hand guide us
       or the randomness of atoms?

No matter, we are here.

And have been naming the names of God, since first we
  Came: Cedar and Cattail, Sweet Grass and Pine, Ash,
   Oak; *Tawatsaako, Maazi, Hante Sha*—fruit of the earth
    for horse's cough, twigs for burning, leaves for draught,
     first tree before man, for lodge pole, for thunder
     forest of thunderbird.

Kirit-tacharush, eye itch of flying down, for pillow, for talc.
  Kataaru for perfume. *Wachanga* to burn evil away.
   Nahata-pahat, Buude-hi for the bowels, *Uta* or *Kiditako*,
   Tashnanga-hi, Rak and *Psehti, Franxinius Marsh*
    for the mystic ash, whose stem draws Pawnee smoke.

Which, if ceasing to be, would be
  like the stars pinched at night,
    snuffing from our eyes all
      that makes us human.

How fast we are gone. How quick we come.
  How we invent and name.

For it rises out of us as we rise out of it as that something
  that crawled from the unctuous unconscious mud
    and wended its way to speak and is speaking still.

One hundred years on the death of Walt, dear
  tender father sweet mother man,
    his tongue

"My tongue, every atom of my blood, formed from this soil,
  this air in my mouth forever."

To love, to be conscious, to honor and have honor,
  to attend, and endure, and preserve,

Say 3,000 years of Alerce trees
  unstumped and still standing.